KATIE

The Little Girl Who Stuttered and Then Learned to Talk Fluently

RONALD L WEBSTER

Copyright © 2012 Ronald L Webster
All rights reserved.

ISBN: 1468004905
ISBN-13: 9781468004908

Six-year-old Katie loved to go to the neighborhood park, play on the jungle gym, and join the other kids in a game of hide-and-seek. Her favorite hiding spot was behind the trunk of an old oak tree. The park was a place she enjoyed and where she could forget about the way she talked.

Ever since she could remember, Katie stuttered. She stuttered when she talked to her mother and her father. She stuttered when she spoke on the telephone with her grandmother. And, she stuttered with her friends.

Sometimes she got stuck on trying to begin a word. When she wanted to say, "I want some ice cream, please," she got stuck on the "I" and couldn't get the sound to come out.

Sometimes her sounds and words got repeated: "He----he---he tried to g-g-g-give me i-i-i-ice cr-cr-cr-cream."

Katie would struggle and struggle to talk. It seemed to take forever to say the simplest things.

At the park playing hide-and-seek, Katie didn't have to talk. She could duck behind the big oak tree and forget about her stuttering.

Katie's mom and dad were concerned about her speech, and they knew how frustrated she felt every time she tried to talk. They took her to see lots of different doctors to improve her stuttering. Yet none of the doctors helped her—though they had some strange things to say.

Some doctors said she might be anxious around people, which caused her to stutter. Katie thought that was silly. She liked people. What she didn't like was stuttering when she tried to talk.

One doctor said her mom and dad were putting pressure on her to be perfect. Katie knew that was not so. She knew her parents loved her just the way she was.

Some doctors even said Katie was not very smart. But Katie was a fast and good learner. She could play a tune on the piano after only a couple of lessons. And she was already reading books that were way ahead of her age.

When it was time to start first grade, Katie looked forward to meeting new friends and having fun. But on the first day, some of the children laughed at her stuttering and made fun of the way she talked.

One girl, Susie, made fun of her by imitating her stuttered speech. Another child, Frank, simply said, "You are stupid," and ran away after sticking his tongue out at her.

Some of Katie's classmates did become friends. They didn't care that she stuttered. Still, day after day when Katie went to school, she was made fun of for the way she talked. Each day it was harder and harder for her to go to school and face the teasing. All she could think about was going to the park after school and hiding behind the big oak tree.

One morning before school, Katie's mom turned on the television and saw a doctor being interviewed on a news show. He was explaining how stuttering could be treated successfully. The doctor showed videos of how this stuttering therapy helped older children and young adults to speak without stuttering.

After watching the interview with her mom, Katie was determined to do something about her stuttering. She asked her mom to call the doctor's office to learn more. She thought, "This is the doctor I need to see." Her mom agreed and made an appointment.

From their home in New York City, Katie and her mother flew to Roanoke, Virginia, to see the doctor. When they met with him, the doctor told Katie that her stuttering was not her fault or her parents' fault.

"Stuttering just happens in some children," he explained. He assured her that children who stutter are just like other kids—they just happen to have trouble talking.

Both the doctor and his assistant talked with Katie. They asked her to answer a lot of questions. She was asked to read from a book. She was so proud that she could read the story, even though she had never seen it before, but she still stuttered.

The doctor asked Katie to say some simple words while she stretched the first sound in each word like "mmmmy" for the word, my, and "rrrrrun" for the word, run. He also asked her to take a breath of air before she stretched some other words. Then, to her surprise, Katie was asked to say a few words to a computer while she started each word with a stretched sound and gentle voice. When she did, a green light came on.

Katie finished all the tests. The doctor told her that she was ready for his stuttering therapy program.

Two weeks later, Katie and her mom flew back to Roanoke to begin therapy. Right away, Katie showed the doctor that she was a good listener and a good learner. The doctor told Katie that they were going to work on learning new ways of talking. He said that her speech muscles were jumping out of control and that he would teach her how to use her muscles differently to control the way she talked. Finally, he told her about "targets," which are ways of creating speech sounds that make smooth speech happen.

During the first week of therapy, Katie learned how to put her mouth in just the right position for starting each sound. She discovered that there were targets for four kinds of sounds she used when she talked. Some were called vowels and sounded like a, e, i, o, and u. Some were stretchy sounds like m, n, l, v, r, and th. And some sounds were filled with air, like f, sh, s, and h. She also learned that some sounds were little pops, like p, b, d, t, ga, and ka.

While Katie knew all the sounds, she had to learn how to control her muscles to say them smoothly. That meant she had to move her tongue, lips, and jaw to just the right position. She also needed to control the way she turned on her voice when beginning to speak.

During therapy, Katie started by saying short words with stretchy sounds. She said, "nnnnight" and "llllove." She also spoke lots of other short words using stretch sounds. They included words like, my, mine, shoe, boat, car, fish and many, many more. It was fun because her words were not getting stuck anymore when she tried to speak. Soon she began to use stretchy sounds with longer words—and again she spoke smoothly without stuttering. Katie also learned how to take a full tummy breath before she started to speak.

She discovered that when she talked to the computer and gently turned on her voice, the green light came on. When she didn't do it right, the computer screen stayed dark. It didn't take long before Katie made the computer light up every time she talked. The doctor was very pleased with how well she was doing.

In her therapy sessions, Katie learned how to make sounds and words all over again. This time her stretchy sounds got shorter, her tummy breath was faster, and her voice control got better with practice on longer words. Katie also practiced talking with the doctor, his assistant, and her mother while using her new way of talking.

One day, Katie was riding to lunch with her mother when she saw a stop sign. She said out loud, "I saw the sign. It said stop. I saw it and I said it! I saw it and I said it!" She did not stutter at all!

Katie read signs to and from the restaurant, and each time she said, "I saw it and I said it! I saw it and I said it!" Her mother was thrilled with her new ability to speak so smoothly.

That evening Katie called her father in New York City. For the first time, her words came out easily with no stutter. She told her dad about all the signs she saw and said. Katie's father was amazed. He listened to his daughter and tears came to his eyes. He was so happy. "I'm so proud of you," he said. He could hardly believe what he was hearing.

Katie and her mother went out for ice cream after the phone call. Katie asked her mother if she could order for herself. She stepped up to the counter and said to the lady, "I would like to have a strawberry ice cream cone, please." The lady never knew Katie stuttered.

Katie continued working hard during therapy. She practiced her new speaking skills with people on the telephone, went to stores and talked with the clerks, and gave speeches to the other people who were in therapy with her. Each day, it became easier and easier to remember to use her targets. Soon, Katie knew that she could talk to anybody she wanted to talk to.

When Katie returned home, she could hardly wait to go back to school. The next morning she skipped into her classroom, ran up to her friends, and started talking. They were amazed to hear her speak. Her stutter was gone. No one laughed or teased her. Instead, they listened to her talk smoothly.

After school, Katie asked her mom to take her to the park. She wanted to climb the jungle gym and play hide-and-seek like she had done so many times before.

When she saw the familiar oak tree, she began to smile. Instead of hiding behind the trunk, she began to climb the tree. When she got halfway up, she called out, "I'm so happy! I love the way I talk!"

Katie had learned how to talk all over again. It was like having a new present every day!

There is more to this story.

It happened after Katie grew up, got married, moved to a far away country, and had a daughter of her own.

Please turn the page to learn more about Katie.

Here is an actual letter that Dr. Webster received from Katie many years after her therapy at Hollins Communications Research Institute (HCRI).

Katie: All Grown Up

Dear Dr. Webster,

I want to share with you something that happened with my daughter, Anna. Two weeks before her third birthday, she manifested all the signs of being a stutterer—an extremely severe stutterer *just like me*. Anna became increasingly angry and frustrated by her inability to get her words out. In a short period of time, her tears and anger escalated into an unrelenting emotional trauma.

As you can imagine, my heart was breaking, as I was certain I was watching myself thirty years earlier. I was determined to teach her the skills I was taught at your institute. I began by explaining to her over and over about how to breathe to help her talk. I taught her about the speech targets. When I spoke, I used the exaggerated speaking manner required to develop and practice fluency skills.

Anna's third birthday came and went. She understood the mechanics of what she needed to do. Yet her stuttering got worse, as did her crying and anger. I could feel her vocal folds shut tight. Facial twitching started and then she stopped talking altogether out of frustration. It was heartbreaking to see someone so little grappling with such loss of muscle control.

Yet I kept working with her and working with her. By Anna's fourth birthday, we had a breakthrough. She started to talk more. I could hear her practicing her breathing on her own. I saw her practice targets in a near whisper, while alone with her dolls. And there was no more facial twitching. The progress continued. By Anna's fifth birthday, she was speaking fluently.

From the beginning, my pain came from knowing deeply how much a life can be swallowed up and manipulated by a severe stutter. I did not want this impediment to be a factor in Anna's life. Above all, I did not want to be the one passing this down, with all its problems, into a sweet new and wide-eyed life.

Today, speech is not an issue for my daughter. I am writing to share what I felt I was able to accomplish because of you and your therapy program. Thank you for helping me give my daughter the best gift of all—complete fluency.

Best wishes always,

Katie

To learn more about the practical,
effective treatment of stuttering, please contact:

Hollins Communications Research Institute
Stuttering Treatment Center
7851 Enon Drive
Roanoke, Virginia 24019

Toll-Free Telephone: 1-855-236-7032

Email: info@stuttering.org

Website: www.stuttering.org